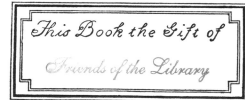

NATURE PROJECTS FOR EVERY SEASON

SUMMER

by Phyllis S. Busch

illustrated by Megan Halsey

BENCHMARK BOOKS

MARSHALL CAVENDISH
NEW YORK

For my dear friends
Lucille Tegg and Doris Stroh
— P. S. B.

To my mother
— M. H.

Benchmark Books
Marshall Cavendish Corporation
99 White Plains Road
Tarrytown, NY 10591-9001

Printed in Hong Kong

First Edition

Library of Congress Cataloging-in-Publication Data
Busch, Phyllis S.
Summer / by Phyllis S. Busch ; illustrated by Megan Halsey.
p. . cm. — (A year of science and nature activities)
Includes bibliographical references (p.) and index.
Summary: Describes changes that occur in nature in summer and suggests activities
that can be used to study what happens to plants and animals at this time of year.
ISBN 0-7614-0987-4
1. Nature study—Activity programs—Juvenile literature. 2. Science—Study and teaching—Activity programs—Juvenile literature.
3. Summer—Juvenile literature. [1. Nature study. 2. Summer.] I. Halsey, Megan, ill. II. Title. III. Series.
QH81.B9936   1999   508.2—dc21   98-53326   CIP   AC

CONTENTS

INTRODUCTION

Seasons change because the earth leans to one side as it travels around the sun. The part of the earth where we live tilts more toward the sun this season of the year than at any other time. This tilt gives us our summer, when we have longer days and shorter nights. Warmer and sunnier days makes summer the warmest season of the year. The longest day arrives about June 21. Summer lasts about thirteen weeks.

The long warm sunny days of summer makes this a great time of the year because so many things are happening outdoors—there's so much for you to see and to do.

You can look for the homes of birds, woodchucks, spiders, and grasshoppers. You can see spiderwebs as well as the froghopper's spittle on stems of plants. Then there are the different kinds of trees, now dressed with leaves of all sorts of shapes. And what can we find out about rocks and wind and clouds? Summer is a great time to enjoy all sorts of science and nature projects.

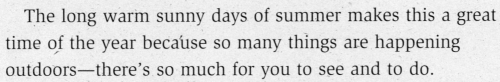

OUTDOOR ACTIVITIES

RECOGNIZING POISON IVY

You will enjoy your outdoor activities more if you learn to avoid things that may be harmful.

Some things are harmful if eaten. Do not put anything in your mouth unless you are told that it is safe by a responsible adult.

Avoid insects that sting such as bees and wasps.

Some plants are harmful to touch. One such plant is poison ivy. It grows in many places. You can find it in the woods, in gardens, and along sides of roads. Learn to recognize it.

Poison ivy may grow as a vine, climbing up a tree or over a fence. It may look like a shrub or a low plant. The leaves may be shiny or dull. They are green, but young leaves are often red colored. The important thing to look for is how the leaves are arranged. They always come in groups of three.

The plant produces white berries in the fall. Birds eat them and remain unharmed but it is poisonous for people to do so. Try to remember this little verse: "Leaves three, quickly flee! Berries white, dreadful sight!"

Many harmless plants also have leaves that grow in threes, such as strawberries. However, if you are not sure, don't touch them.

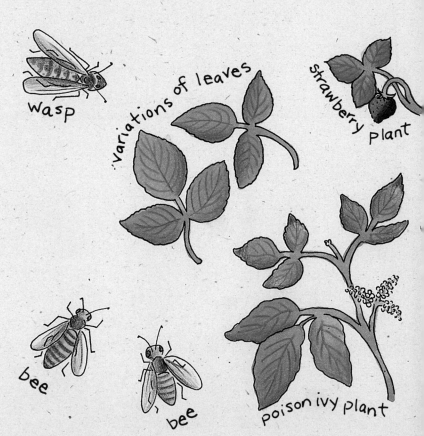

wasp

Variations of leaves

strawberry plant

bee

bee

poison ivy plant

SPITTING INSECTS

Look for little white masses of froth on the stems of grasses and other plants. The froth is not spit. It only looks like spit. Each mass is the home of a tiny immature insect called a spittlebug.

The spittlebug feeds on the juices of stems. It also uses the sap to build its moist home. It is perfectly safe to remove some froth with your finger to find the insect. It is very small, soft, and pale green.

Place the spittlebug gently on another part of the plant stem. Wait a few minutes. It will turn head down and sink its mouth into the plant. It begins to suck the plant juices at once.

Even as the insect is feeding, bubbles of froth appear from its opposite end. It is building another home. It will live inside this white mass until it becomes an adult.

The adult is found toward the end of the summer. It continues to feed on the sap of plants but it stops building bubble houses. The adult is a little brown insect that hops somewhat like a frog. It is now called a froghopper.

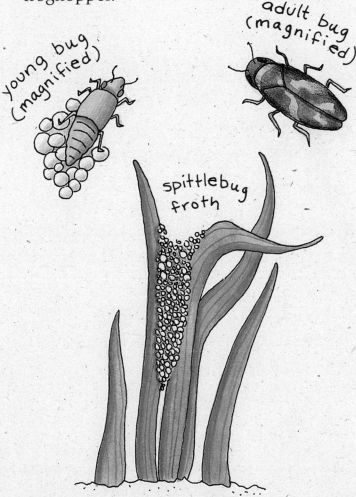

young bug (magnified)

adult bug (magnified)

spittlebug froth

A FEEL WALK

You can learn a great deal about things by touching them. Plan to take a walk wherever you like to be. You might choose a woodland, a garden, a roadside, or a vacant lot. There are many things to touch and feel wherever you go.

Start your feel walk by touching leaves. Be sure not to touch leaves that are poisonous. Find as many different kinds of leaves as you can. Feel the edges of the leaves. They may be sharp or smooth or wavy. Touch the surface of leaves. They may be smooth, sticky, fuzzy, or prickly. Feel the tips of leaves. How are the tips of some leaves different from the rest of the leaf?

Rub your hand on the bark of trees. Bark may be smooth or rough.

Rub some soil between your fingers. Test soil from different spots. Soils may feel sandy, gritty, or sticky.

Feel some rocks and pebbles. They may be sharp, rough, or smooth.

Are there differences in the feel of some grasses? Grass may feel dry, damp, warm, or cool.

When you have finished your walk, just stand still. Hold your face and hands up to feel the wind, the sun, the shade.

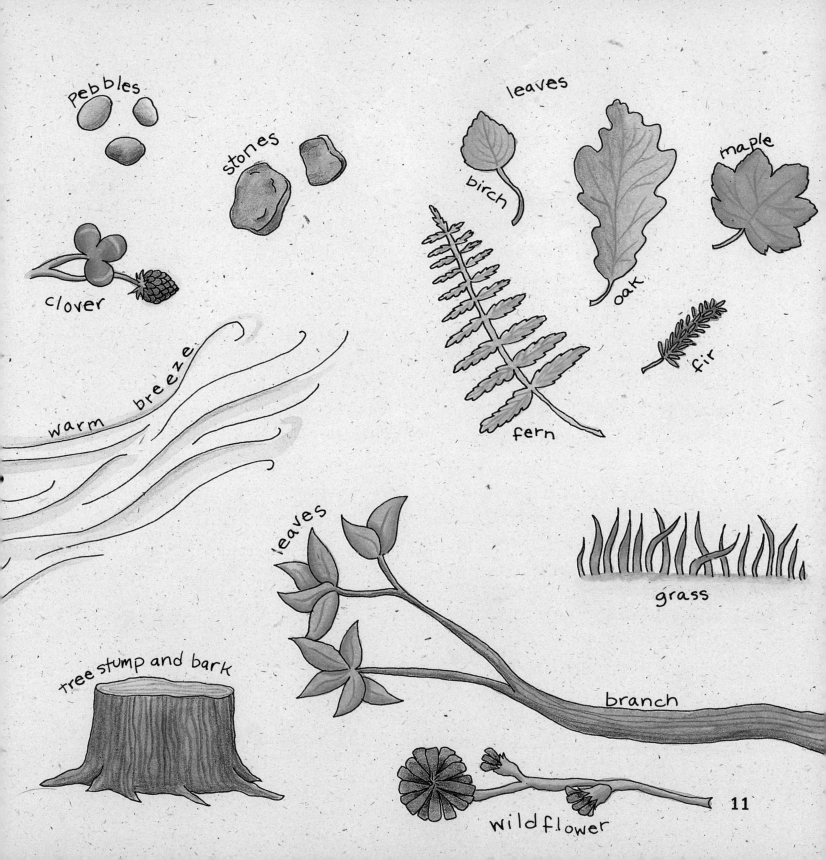

pebbles

stones

clover

warm breeze

leaves

birch

oak

maple

fern

fir

leaves

grass

tree stump and bark

branch

wildflower

11

LIVING FLASHLIGHTS

Twilight is the time of day after the sun has set and before it gets dark. Summer has long periods of twilight. Go outdoors in early summer after the sun sets to see fireflies beginning to blink. You will find them above the grass of meadows, gardens, or roadsides.

The males are sending signals to attract females. The light of the firefly is a cold light. It looks like a little lantern hanging down from the back end of the insect's body.

The males blink three or four times as they fly above the grass. They rest a while and then blink the same number of times again. Females return their signal while waiting on the ground. Blinking stops when the insects meet and mate. The females lay their eggs in the ground after mating. These eggs will produce a new generation of fireflies next year.

You can collect enough fireflies to make a living flashlight. Find out how many of these insects you need in order to have enough light for reading. You will need a small jar with a lid. Make some holes in the lid for air to enter the jar. Take along a piece of newspaper and see if you have enough fireflies to read it. Release the fireflies after about an hour.

You can also take a regular flashlight with you and try to copy the signals of a blinking firefly. Perhaps one will mistake you for a female firefly and pay you a surprise visit.

fireflies

12

SPIDERWEBS

Spiderwebs are among the most beautiful things in nature. They look best in the very early morning when the dew is still on the webs. Webs become almost invisible when the dew evaporates. Take a small garden sprayer filled with water if you go hunting for spiderwebs later in the day. Find a web and stand in front of it. Spray the web very gently with a fine mist of water. The web will glisten as if it were covered with morning dew.

Spiderwebs are made of silk. A spider's body is like a little silk factory. It has liquid inside that the spider can spin into threads. The liquid is pushed out through special little openings at the end of its body. First the spider attaches to twigs. Then the spider weaves the rest of the web. Spiders use their webs to catch their food, which is mainly insects.

One of the most beautiful webs is made by the yellow and black garden spider. There is an easy way to collect one of these webs. Do this on a clear windless day. First you will need a can of white spray paint and a piece of dark construction paper. Spray the web on both sides then catch the web on the paper. Let it dry for a few minutes. You now have a permanent web. The spider will make a new one the next day.

a spider's web

13

CLOUD PICTURES

Summer is the best season for watching the sky. The morning sky may be clear and cloudless. Then clouds begin to appear and grow larger during the day. This is a good day to observe the sky. Take along a blanket to lie on, and find a comfortable open spot to enjoy a sky view above.

Watch the large fluffy white clouds. Can you think of some other words to describe them? How about words such as "puffy" or "white cotton candy"? If the clouds are a little darker at the bottom, it will probably continue to be fair weather.

Notice the movement of the clouds. Clouds are piled up in layers and the layers of clouds are always moving. Notice that some layers move in one direction while others move in the opposite direction. This movement is caused by winds. Some people believe that if clouds move in opposite directions it will rain in a few hours.

The fluffy white summer clouds are thousands of feet in the air. Moist air from the earth becomes cooler as it rises. Water droplets form as the air cools. Raindrops fall when the cloud of water droplets become too heavy.

The clouds are forever changing their shapes. That's when you can see all kinds of figures in them. The figures are also constantly changing. You can imagine that they are doing something. In fact, you can make up a story about what you imagine is happening in the cloud pictures. Compare your story to those made up by friends as you watch the same clouds.

MALE AND FEMALE BIRDS

Birds are either male or female. The female is the mother bird. She lays the eggs that hatch into baby birds. The male is the father bird. The males of some birds have more colorful feathers than the females. This is true of the robin, the house sparrow, the bluebird, and the cardinal. However, the feathers of male blue jays, crows, and pigeons are the same as those of the females.

Watch some summer birds and learn to recognize the differences between the two sexes. A good place to watch them would be at a bird feeder. You can also attract birds by throwing some birdseed on the ground.

The male cardinal has bright red feathers with a black throat. Its mate is yellow-brown with a few touches of red. Both have thick red beaks and pointed crests on the top of their heads.

The male robin is brighter than his mate. He has a black head, a brown back and a bright brick-red breast. The mother bird has a paler back and breast and no black feathers on her head.

Bluebirds do not usually come to feeders. They do come to bluebird

male cardinal

male robin

male bluebird

nesting boxes provided for them. Bluebirds have sky-colored feathers on their backs and earth-colored ones on their breasts. The male's head, back, tail, and wings are bright blue. Its breast is red. The female is paler with only a little pale red color on its breast.

The house sparrow is found everywhere, especially in cities. The male is attractively colored. His head is gray on top with reddish patches on both sides. He has a black bib that makes him easily recognized. His back feathers are brown with black streaks. The female is much paler and lacks the black bib.

There are ways of recognizing the differences between the sexes of birds even when their feathers are the same. You can observe how they behave and decide which is male and which is female. This difference is easy to see as you watch pigeons. Male pigeons frequently follow female pigeons. Male chickadees remove the seed coats from sunflower seeds and present them to female chickadees. The males of white-breasted nuthatches also present sunflower seeds to the females during courtship. Can you observe differences in the behavior of other birds where the male and females look alike?

male house sparrow male pigeon male chickadee

HABITATS: WHERE PLANTS AND ANIMALS LIVE

Every plant and animal is at home in its HABITAT. We could say this in another way. Every plant and animal is at home in its NEIGHBORHOOD. A proper habitat provides the right conditions for living things to survive. The necessary conditions are the right temperature, enough food, water, air, and protection from enemies.

Some habitats where you can find plants and animals are fields, streams, woodlands, gardens, ponds, caves, and soil. These are large habitats.

Smaller habitats are places such as living trees, dead trees that are standing, logs on the ground, the foam on a blade of grass, a puddle of water. You will also find life under a rock, in a curled-up leaf, or even in a hole in a twig.

Decide on one or more habitats that you would like to explore. Make several trips to that neighborhood and keep a list of what you see. Try to figure out how the plants or animals get what they need in order to survive.

a garden habitat

a pond habitat

life in and on a log

a field habitat

life under a rock

a stream habitat

JUMPING GRASSHOPPERS

One does not notice grasshoppers unless they jump. Their colors blend with the background and this makes them hard to see. Grasshoppers have very strong hind legs and can jump long distances. They can leap twenty times their body length with one push.

The insect at rest lies quietly with its wings folded and hidden. The wings open when the grasshopper flies.

It would be interesting to find out how many times a grasshopper can leap before it becomes too tired to continue. You will need a clean can or small jam jar in which to place one or two grasshoppers. The container should have a cover with some air holes so that the insect can breathe.

The best way to collect grasshoppers is to use an insect net. Sweep the net through long grass or tall plants. Put the collected insects in your container and take them to a place where the ground is bare or paved. Free one of them. It may not jump at once. Touch it gently with a stick if it does not jump. How many times does the grasshopper jump before it becomes too tired to continue?

You can also measure the distance the grasshopper jumps. Place a stone at the place where it lands each time. You can measure the distance with a ruler when you are through.

Replace any remaining grasshoppers in a grassy area.

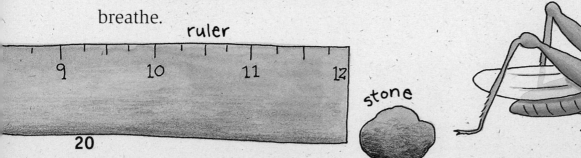

ruler

9 10 11 12

20

stone

grasshopper

LEAVES LOSE WATER

Tree leaves act as little factories, manufacturing food for the tree. In order to carry on this work, they need energy from the sun, as well as a gas called carbon dioxide. This gas is in the air. It enters the leaves through tiny openings. As a result of all this manufacturing, which is called photosynthesis, the leaves give off oxygen and water.

Oxygen freshens the air that we breathe. The water that comes out of the leaf is invisible. It becomes visible as clouds when it reaches the cooler air up above.

You can see this water that comes out from leaves down here on earth. All you need are some plastic baggies and some twist ties. Get about ten of each and go outdoors on a sunny day. This will also work pretty well on a cloudy day, although more foodmaking takes place on sunny days than on cloudy ones.

Therefore more water will be given off by the leaves on days when the sun shines.

Select some tree leaves that you can reach. Using a twist tie, tie a baggie around each leaf that you have selected. Test leaves that are in the sun and leaves in the shade. Test leaves on different kinds of trees. Test some dead leaves. Fasten some of the baggies around twigs without leaves. You will see water collected in the baggies in about fifteen minutes. Leave some baggies on overnight or longer.

You can measure the amount of water from each leaf by emptying the baggie into a measuring cup. What kind of tree produced the most water?

branch

leaf

leaf

bag

water

TREE LEAVES

There are many different kinds of trees. The leaves of each kind of tree has its own special shape. You can learn to recognize trees from the shapes of their leaves.

Place a piece of tracing paper over the drawings of the leaf shapes in your book. Trace the outlines with a pencil. Fasten your copy to a piece of cardboard to make it firm. Take your drawings and a pencil with you to places where trees are growing. Match the leaves of each tree to one of your pictures.

You will notice that some trees have relatives growing in the same neighborhood. Their leaves are somewhat different from each other. For example, you may find oak trees whose leaves have rounded edges, and oak trees whose leaves have sharp edges. This could be true of maple trees and birch trees too.

Examine the leaves carefully to see any differences.

There are books where you can learn more about identifying trees. [One is listed on page 46.]

tulip

birch

birch

poplar

ash

maple

maple

dogwood

oak

oak

cherry

sassafras

sassafras

locust

23

WOODCHUCKS

Woodchucks are either eating or sleeping. They go to sleep at the beginning of October and wake up in the spring. As soon as they awaken they begin to feed. After such a long winter nap, they're hungry!

You can see these brown chunky bearlike animals wherever their favorite food grows. They feed on grass, clover, or vegetables and are often found in people's vegetable gardens. You can also see them in grassy roadside places.

Woodchucks eat twice a day at the beginning of the summer, in the morning and in the evening. They begin to feed all day long toward the end of summer. This is when they are trying to get fat in order to survive their long winter nap.

Woodchucks live in burrows that they dig near their food supply. They can then run and hide if they are scared. You will see the wood-chuck stand up straight and look around as you approach it. It may suddenly dive into its burrow.

Try to find a woodchuck's burrow. Look near a fence or a heap of stones. The burrow has a pile of soil heaped up at the entrance. Somewhere nearby are also two or more escape routes with hidden openings, without a pile of soil.

Suppose you find a burrow but do not see the woodchuck. You could find out if anyone is home. Roll a small stone into the burrow. You will hear the sound of digging if someone is inside. The woodchuck is throwing up a wall of earth before it dashes out through one of its secret exits.

fence

pile of soil

escape route

escape route

burrow

CAN YOU FIND IT?

Take a nature walk to find and collect the things on this list. If the item is too large or if you cannot collect it, write a few words to describe it. Make a copy of this list and check off each item you find. You will need a collecting bag, paper, and pencil. Remember to look up in the sky, straight ahead, and on the ground.

1. Something green
2. Something brown
3. Something gray
4. Something blue
5. Something that is not natural and does not belong here
6. A feather
7. A dead twig
8. An ant
9. A flower in bloom
10. A flower that has finished blooming
11. An insect
12. The footprint of an animal with four legs
13. A spider or a spiderweb
14. A natural item that is being recycled
15. Three little stones, each of a different size, shape, and color
16. The shape of a cloud
17. A tree leaf that is moving
18. A leaf with wavy edges
19. The sound of a bird
20. Proof that the wind is blowing

How many more observations of your own can you make?

INDOOR ACTIVITIES

WATER FROM THE SOIL TRAVELS UP INTO LEAVES

Plants use soil water in order to make food. The water from the soil enters the roots of plants and then travels up the stems into the leaves. You can demonstrate this very easily. You will need six clear bottles or glasses, some red and green food coloring, water, two white carnations, and two celery stalks with their leaves attached.

Fill two containers half full of water. Add the red food color to each. Place a celery stalk in one and a carnation in the other. You can see the red color in the celery leaves and in the carnation in a few days.

Now try to make a two-colored carnation and celery leaves. Fill the remaining four bottles half full of water. Color the water in two of them with the red food coloring and two with the green.

Ask an adult to cut the celery and the flower lengthwise about half way up their stalks. Put half of the carnation stem into red water and the other half into green. Do the same with the celery. The white flower will turn half red and half green. The celery stalk and leaves will also show two colors.

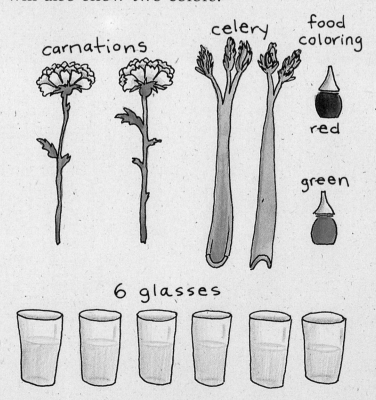

carnations   celery   food coloring

red

green

6 glasses

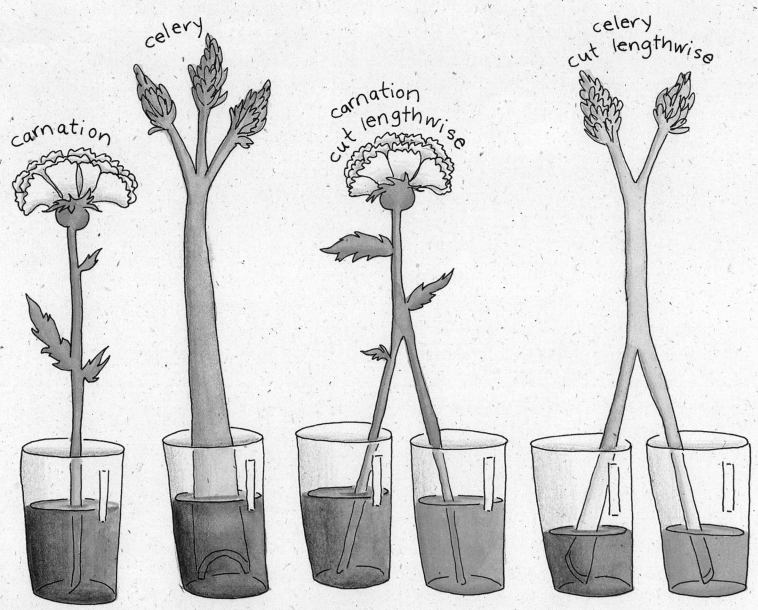

carnation

celery

carnation cut lengthwise

celery cut lengthwise

colored water that will travel up the stems

YOU CAN HAVE FUN RECYCLING USED THINGS

Be an inventor. Figure out how you can change trash into something useful. For example, take an empty milk carton. Wash it and take time to look at it. How can you recycle it? Can you think of a way to make it into a toy apartment house by cutting out doors and windows? How could you use it for growing plants? Decorate it and use it as a pencil holder. Think of other ways in which to use empty milk cartons. Make it attractive and give it as a gift.

How can you change a discarded soap dish to a suet feeder for birds?

Think of all the useful things you can make from empty plastic bleach containers of different sizes. Here are a few ideas: a funnel, a scoop, a bird feeder, a vase, a flower pot.

Glass bottles of different shapes and sizes can be turned into pretty flower vases. Clean the jar and dry it well. Prepare a shallow dish with a thin layer of plain or colored sand. Paint the outside of the jar with glue. Carefully roll the jar in the sand and let it dry.

How many uses can you make of an egg carton? These are good for collections of things such as stones, beads, buttons, small treasures.

When you recycle used objects you are using your brain to be creative. You are also preventing waste. And you are having fun.

milk carton pencil holder

a toy apartment house

jar

glue

colored sand

stones   buttons   treasures

a scoop

egg carton

flower pot   markers

31

HOW FAST DOES WATER EVAPORATE?

Pour a fourth of a cup of water into a measuring cup. Place it on a windowsill and look at it each day. You will see that the water gradually disappears until there is no more water left in the cup. The water has changed to water vapor, which is an invisible gas. The vapor became part of the air. This process is called evaporation.

Pour the same amount of water into four cups or glasses of the same size. Place one on a sunny windowsill. Place another on another windowsill where there is no sun. A third should be put near a stove or other source of heat. Place the fourth in the refrigerator. Do not cover them.

Try to figure out the order in which the water will evaporate from the glasses. Which will lose all its water first? second? third? fourth? You will find out by examining the water left in the glasses every day until complete evaporation has taken place in all of them. You will see that water evaporates faster where it is warmer because warm air can hold more water vapor than cold air.

SQUEEZING WATER OUT OF THE AIR

The water in the air is in the form of an invisible gas that we call water vapor. You can easily make this gas come out of the air as drops of water. Fill a glass with ice water. Place the glass where it is warm. Any place will do on a hot summer day.

After a while you will notice the drops of water on the outside of the glass. The cold inside the glass cooled the glass as well as the air around it. The cold air that forms around the glass cannot hold as much water vapor as warm air. The cold air temperature therefore changed the water vapor to drops of water.

GREEN PLANTS NEED SUNLIGHT

All green plants need sunlight in order to make food. Some need more light than others. What happens when you take sunlight away from a plant? Can it recover? Here is one way to find out.

Get a geranium plant. Geraniums require sunlight on their broad green leaves. You will also need a piece of black construction paper, a pair of scissors, a pencil, a quarter or a large button, and some paper clips or wooden clothespins.

Place the plant in a sunny window. Be sure it is well watered. Cut out some little black circles from the construction paper. Make them about as large as a quarter. You can place the coin (or button) on the paper, trace a circle around it, and then cut out a circle. You will probably need about ten circles.

Select several of the largest leaves. Gently fasten two paper circles to the edge of each leaf that you have selected. Use either a paper fastener or a clothespin for each circle. Do not bruise the leaves.

Remove the papers very carefully after leaving them on for a week. The color of the leaf under the papers was faded. It is yellow instead of green. The leaves are unable to make food without the green substance. Leave the plant where it is and continue to take care of it. Does the green come back? The green substance in the leaves is called chlorophyll. How long does it take the geranium to recover its chlorophyll?

Watering can

paper clips or clothespin

geranium plant

black paper

black paper circles clipped on the leaf

quarter or button

Pencil

Scissors

35

EXAMINE SOME "FLOWER DUST"

Many flowers bloom in the summer. Collect a few to keep in some water indoors. Look inside the flowers. Most of them have yellow centers. Some have other colors. Run your finger over the centers and you will notice that some of the color comes off on your finger. This is sometimes called "flower dust." It is pollen, a substance produced by flowers. Plants need pollen in order to make seeds.

Each kind of flower develops pollen of a different shape and design. How many different kinds of pollen grains can you find? You will need a magnifier in order to see the pollen clearly. You will also need some glass slides like those used under a microscope or you can use small plastic lids. You should also have a pad and pencil.

Shake a blossom over one of the slides or lids. If nothing comes off, try rubbing your finger gently over the center of the blossom, and then touching the slide or lid. You can also try using a small paint brush to collect the pollen from the flower.

Examine the pollen grains from different flowers with your magnifier. If possible, look at them under a microscope. You will be astonished at the variety and beauty of pollen grains. Each kind looks like a miniature piece of sculpture. Make some drawings of what you see. Write the name of the flower next to each kind of pollen.

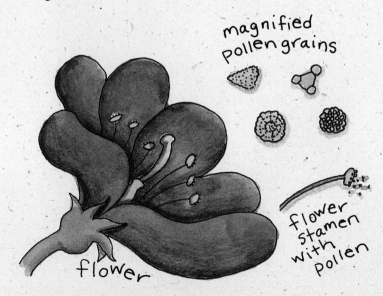

magnified pollen grains

flower

flower stamen with pollen

HOW DO INSECTS STAY ON TOP OF THE WATER?

Have you ever watched insects darting about on the surface of a pond? How do they remain on top? What prevents them from drowning? You can find out with a glass of water and a box of nails. Get a small box of nails called carpet tacks. They have flat heads and short stems.

Place the glass of water on a table. How many tacks do you think you can drop into the water before the water flows over the edge of the glass?

Drop in one tack at a time. Hold the tack by its pointed end. First dip the head below the surface of the water, then drop the tack.

Look at the edge of the glass after you have put in quite a few tacks. Can you see the water bulge in the middle? The water rises higher as you drop in more tacks. It looks as if the water has a skin that is stretching.

Water that is covered by air forms a tight membrane. This membrane, or water skin, keeps the insects on the surface of a pond from drowning.

You can do the same thing with dimes instead of tacks, You will be surprised at the number of dimes you can drop into a glass of water.

Try to float a sewing needle on top of the water. Lay it down slowly to prevent breaking the surface of the water.

PLAY WITH DROPS OF WATER

Water is very important. It is also very interesting. You can learn much about it by playing with just a few drops of water.

Place the following items on a tray: a small bowl of water, a pinch of powered detergent, a small piece of soap, a birthday candle, a wooden pencil, a piece of wax paper, a piece of paper towel, and a piece of news-paper. The three pieces of paper should be about half the size of this page.

Dip your fingers into the bowl of water and shake them over the wax paper. This will produce drops of different sizes. Shake some water on the paper towel and on the newspa-per. How are the shapes of the drops different on the three papers?

Push the drops of water together on the wax paper to see if they join to form one larger drop.

What happens to the drop if you add a pinch of detergent to it?

What happens to a water drop if you touch it with a piece of soap?

Does the water climb up the pencil when it is dipped into a drop?

Place the wax paper over the news-print. A drop acts as a magnifier. Do larger drops make the letters appear larger than smaller drops?

These are but a few things you can do. Think of others you might try. You can color the water to make drops that resemble different gems. Try drawing on a water drop with an old-style pen and liquid ink. What are some of the interesting things you learned about water?

soap

bowl of water

birthday candle

pencil

detergent

wax paper

paper towel

newspaper

39

WATER PLANTS NEED SUNLIGHT

All leaves need energy from sunlight to make plant food no matter where they live. Some leaves, such as the leaves of trees and roses, live in the air. Some float on top of the water, such as the leaves of pond lilies and water lilies. There are some water plants that grow entirely underwater, the kinds of plants that could grow in fish tanks.

How do such water plants get energy from the sun? Sunlight shines through water. The leaves reached by sunlight can use the sun's energy to make food. More sunlight can shine through clear water than through muddy water. From which water areas would plants get the most sunlight?

Collect some water samples in small jars from several different places. Try to get water from places such as a pond, a swamp, a stream, a brook, or a river. Be sure to note where you get each sample.

Place the jars on a sunny windowsill. Arrange your samples from the one with the clearest water to the muddiest. Now you can tell in which body of water the water plants could make the most food.

different types of water

LEAF PRINTS

You will enjoy making your own print collection of tree leaves. There are many ways to make leaf prints. Here are two simple methods. First collect several different kinds of leaves. Take two or three from each tree.

1. INK PAD PRINTS For this method you will need a large ink pad and some clean white sheets of paper. Place one leaf at a time on the pad with its underside down against the pad. Cover with a piece of white paper. Cover with another sheet of paper. Hold the paper down with one hand and rub firmly with the fingers of your other hand.

2. LEAF RUBBINGS You will need some fat black wax crayons and some strong white paper, such as tracing paper. Of course you will also need your leaf collection. Remove the paper covering from the crayon. Lay the leaf on a piece of newspaper with its underside up. Place a white sheet of paper on top of the leaf. Rub across the leaf with the side of the crayon. You will see the leaf print on the top sheet of paper. You may wish to practice by first making rubbings of a penny or other coin.

inkpad leaves paper coins crayons

MAKE A BIRD MOBILE

A mobile is a form of art. It is a movable sculpture. Try making a bluebird mobile. You will need a straight plastic drinking straw, scissors, strong thread, a needle, cardboard, paints, crayons or markers, tracing paper, a pencil, an outline of a bluebird.

Place tracing paper over the outline of the bluebird on this page. Trace it with your pencil. Cut out the outline and use it as a pattern to make several bluebird shapes on pieces of cardboard. Cut out the bird shapes and color them. The color of the bluebird is sky blue with a rusty breast.

Thread the needle with a piece of thread about as long as your arm. Draw the thread through the straw. Fasten each end of the thread to a bird shape and tie a knot to keep the bird in place.

Cut another piece of thread to be used as a hanger by tying it as shown on the next page. Hang the mobile where it can move freely. Balance the cutouts so that the straw does not slant but hangs straight. Watch your mobile move.

Can you figure out how to add more cutouts to your mobile? You may want to make a mobile with a collection of different bird pictures. How can you make a feather mobile?

bluebird shape for tracing

drinking straws

paints

crayons

markers

thread

tracing paper

TRACING PAPER

cardboard

needles

needles

pencil

scissors

43

PUT UP A WREN HOUSE

One of the most pleasant sounds in the summer is the bubbling song of the house wren. You can enjoy its music by providing it with a nearby place to nest. It will readily accept a clay flower pot in which to build its nest. Both the pot and the hole have to be the right size. A six-inch (fifteen centimeter) clay pot is just right if its hole is enlarged.

Besides a six-inch clay flower pot, you will need some newspaper, a pencil, a quarter, a screwdriver, a hammer, and three strong nails. Invite an adult to work with you.

Spread some newspaper on a table or the floor. Place the pot on the paper with its rim down and the hole on top. Put the quarter over the hole and draw an outline around the coin.

Using the hammer and screwdriver, enlarge the hole of the pot by chipping the clay away along the line that you drew around the quarter.

Find a place outdoors where you can hammer three nails into wood to support the pot on its side with the hole facing toward you. Choose a tree or the side of an outdoor building such as a garage. [The pot does not have to be any higher than your head] It is easy to remove the nails to clean the pot at the end of the nesting season.

WRITE A LETTER

Write a letter to a friend in which you tell about an indoor or outdoor adventure. Here are some ways to start your letter.

Have you ever seen cloud pictures in the sky?

or

Last week I saw a woodchuck.

or

I learned how to squeeze water out of the air.

or

Do you know why some insects can stay on top of the water?

or

Make up your own beginning sentence.

Perhaps you would like to show a friend some of the outdoor places you have visited. Maybe your friend can join you to make a mobile or a wren house or some other indoor activity that you enjoyed. It's fun to share.

Dear Martin,
Last week I saw a big woodchuck! It's furry and fast! It jumped into its hole in the ground really quickly. I heard it scratching and digging it's way deep into its home.

Dear Olivia and Claire,
Hi! How are you both? I'm well. I found some spittlebugs in my backyard. They make froth on plants. It looks like this.

I found a lot of cool stones and leaves too. I traced these leaves for you.

sassafras

birch

SOME READING SUGGESTIONS

Arnofsky, Jim. *Butterflies and Moths*. New York: Simon and Schuster, 1996.

Asch, Frank. *Sawgrass Poems*. New York: Harcourt Brace and Co., 1996.

Bailey, Jill. *How Spiders Make Their Webs*. New York: Marshall Cavendish, 1997

Lerner, Carol. *Backyard Birds of Summer*. New York: Morrow Junior Books, 1996.

Thompson, Mary. *Gran's Bees*. Brookfield, Conn.: Millbrook Press, 1996.

Wyler, Rose. *Raindrops and Rainbows*. Englewood Cliffs, N.J.: Julian Messner, 1989.

Pine, Jonathan. *Trees*. New York: Harper-Collins Nature Study Services, 1995.

INDEX

Page numbers for illustrations are in boldface

6/00

The Cyrenius H. Booth Library

Newtown, Connecticut

Tel. 426-4533

RULES FOR BORROWERS

Borrowers - Any resident of Newtown may borrow books upon filling an application.

Number of Books - Adults may borrow six books at a time. Children may borrow six books at a time.

Time Kept - Books may be kept for two weeks and renewed for two weeks except seven days books.

Overdue Books - For books kept overtime a fine will be charged according to the rules of the library. A borrower must pay for damage to a book and for replacing a lost book.

DEMCO